We're in Heaven,
and I Have Some Questions

We're in Heaven,
and I Have Some Questions

VANESSA ECHOLS

Archway Publishing books may be ordered through booksellers or by contacting:

Archway Publishing
1663 Liberty Drive
Bloomington, IN 47403
www.archwaypublishing.com
844-669-3957

ISBN: 978-1-6657-2812-6 (sc)
ISBN: 978-1-6657-2813-3 (e)

Library of Congress Control Number: 2022914239

Print information available on the last page.

Archway Publishing rev. date: 08/15/2022

Contents

This book is dedicated to my parents, Hosea and Mary Echols, who have made me feel loved every single day of my life, and who made sure Sunday school was a major part of my childhood. The Bible stories came alive at Mt. Moriah Missionary Baptist Church in Auburn, Alabama, and that is where I started asking questions.

If you don't have a sense of humor, don't read this book. It's not for you. Most authors would not start by telling a group of people not to read her book, but that's exactly what I'm doing. This book is for those of us who believe not only is God okay with us having a sense of humor but also He has one too. If you know me, you'll hear my voice throughout these pages. If you don't know me, you'll be familiar with my voice by the end. So get ready for a few *y'all*s and other things we used to say while growing up in Alabama.

You'll see me refer to the Book. That of course is *the* book, the Bible. And I've chosen to capitalize He and Him when referring to God and Jesus.

I've chosen to tell the stories of forty people because forty is a significant number in the Bible. Jesus, Moses, and Elijah all fasted for forty days. Jesus was tempted for forty days. The Israelites wandered in the wilderness for forty years. Those are just a few examples.

After the end of each chapter, you'll see one final question, Scripture references (not all Scriptures about each person, but some key ones), and a blank page. That's for you to write your own questions and thoughts.

I'm so happy you are on this journey with me. Let's ask some questions.

Abraham

Well, if it isn't Mr. Father of Many Nations himself. I have *so* many questions for you, but they can all pretty much be summed up with this: Dude, what were you thinking? Yes, I realize that crazy plan to have a baby with the maid was Sarah's idea, but you went along with that! You had to know that was not gonna turn out well.

Before all that real-life soap opera stuff, though, you showed us what obedience to God looks like. I see why you are listed in the Faith Hall of Fame in Hebrews 11. You were all settled in, living your best life in Haran. You probably had a custom tent, the latest camel, a pension, and a 401(k). Then God told you to move, but He didn't tell you where. What was that conversation like with Sarah? "Honey, I'm home, and we're moving, and I don't know where we're going." I'm sure the folks at the moving company were like, "Let me get this straight. We're going to load up your stuff, but nobody knows where you're going yet?"

But you obeyed, and God fulfilled every single thing He promised you. Every. Single. One.

Then He really blew your mind when He told you that He was changing your name and was going to make you a daddy. Yes, you a daddy at one hundred, this time with your actual wife, who was also no spring chicken at ninety.

How you must have loved baby Isaac and felt such joy watching him grow. And then God came along and told you to do something none of us can imagine. He told you to kill your own son, the same son He had promised you. I'm guessing you were like, "Wait … what? You want me to do *what*?"

That must have been the most difficult part of your life, going to Moriah and knowing what you were about to do, with Isaac being none the wiser. And I guess you didn't tell Sarah what you were going to do because she would have stood at the door of the tent and tried to block you. But I noticed when you got to Moriah, you told the servants with you that "we" would be back—you and Isaac. You had some kind of confidence, my friend.

Anyway, I've also wondered, when you tied up Isaac and laid him on the wood, what was he doing and saying? Was he struggling, asking why you were doing that, pleading and begging you to stop? Then, just as you had the knife in the air, I can imagine the Hollywood movie music playing and God saying, "Wait!" Whew! Just in the nick of time. There was a ram in the bush to take Isaac's place as the sacrifice. And on the way back home, I'm thinking you and Isaac probably made a pact: Don't tell Mom.

You really had a remarkable life. I just have one final question: After that ram-in-the-bush incident, did Isaac get a little nervous whenever he saw you with a knife?

Abraham's story:

Genesis 11–25

Adam

The original alpha male. I'm sure everyone here wants to meet you. Allow me to be perfectly honest here. Some days I was really mad at you. We could have all been enjoying the good life in the garden if ... well, you know the rest of the story. You were there.

But I'll move on from that. That must have been quite an experience. Just you and the Lord hanging out with nobody else around. And you got to name all the animals. How cool is that!

Then God became your anesthesiologist, knocked you out for a couple of hours, and He performed the first surgery in the history of the world. You woke up, and there was another person. But she didn't look exactly like you. I mean, you both had eyes, ears, arms, legs, and such. But clearly there were some differences. Obviously, you liked what you saw. It was love at first sight.

Now let's chat about that crafty serpent. When Eve ate the fruit, did you try to intervene, or were you just standing around waiting to see what would happen? I've always wondered. Sounds like the original peer pressure to me, because you took a bite too. Your eyes were opened, and that was when the trouble started. Then you and Eve had to grab the sewing kit and make your first couture fig-leaf outfits.

Your blood pressure must have been through the roof in your failed attempt to hide from the Almighty. And then you blamed Eve. Come on, man! Okay, I realize I can't be too hard on you. I have the advantage of seeing what could have been, and it's easy for all of us to say we would have made the right choice. But would we?

So unfortunately, you got an eviction notice from the landlord, the actual Lord. You and Eve had to pack your bags and vacate the premises immediately. You broke your lease, so you probably didn't get back your security deposit, right?

You were forced to be a hard worker and started a family. That brought you some heartbreak too. One son killed the other. You must have had a lot of regret and asked all the what-if questions.

And I have this question for you: How did you come up with the name *hippopotamus*?

Adam's story:

Genesis 2–4

Daniel

Hey there, Mr. Lion Tamer. Pleasure to meet you.

First off, I guess you know you inspired millions of people to go on a Daniel diet/healthy-eating plan of vegetables and water, with some adding a few fruits as well. And let me tell you, it was hard. I tried it a few times, and by the end of the ten days, I was having a dream about chicken wings. Anyway, I admire how you made it look so easy.

But you didn't just have willpower. You showed us what courage looks like too. After interpreting dreams for King Nebuchadnezzar, you were thriving in your administrative role under King Darius's reign. Yup, you were on the fast track to management. He was so impressed that he was probably going to send you to MBA school and everything. But your coworkers got big-time jealous and tried to plot against you. Haters!

Your work ethic was impeccable and spotless, so then they tried to come at you and your commitment to the Lord. They approached the king with a Babylon city ordinance: for the next thirty days, any resident who prayed to any god or human being other than King Darius would be tossed into the lion's den. It obviously appealed to the king's ego, and he put his stamp on the decree and made it official policy.

Uh-oh. But you didn't flinch. You went home, went to your upstairs room where the windows opened toward Jerusalem, got down on your knees, prayed, and continued to do so three times a day. You weren't even the least bit scared, were you?

Well, then the haters—ah, er, I meant to say group of administrators—plotting against you went tattling to the king. The king was conflicted because he did like you. But those midlevel managers gave him the old, "But you had said …" So eventually he followed through and had you tossed into the lion's den.

The king went back to the palace in anguish and had a restless night; he couldn't eat or sleep. He got up early the next morning and took the royal motorcade to the lion's den to check on your fate. The king called out to you, not expecting an answer of course. But lo and behold, you answered. You told the king that the Lord sent an angel to shut the mouths of the lions. You were perfectly fine and, oh, by the way, innocent of the bogus charges against you.

Well, the king was so overwhelmed with this latest turn of events that he had your accusers and their families thrown into the den. Even their families. Clearly the king was not playin'. However, they did not meet the same fate as you. They were buffet of the day for the lions. And King Darius issued a new decree that everybody in his kingdom must fear and revere the God of Daniel.

But I do have one question about the Daniel diet. You didn't want to add in doughnuts, not even for one day?

Daniel's story:

Daniel

David

David! This could take a while. Good thing we have all of eternity to chat.

I loved reading about your story because God described you as a man after His own heart. Even with all your mess-ups, that's what He thought about you. Your life was super fascinating, fascinating enough to be a network TV miniseries. It certainly had all the elements: slaying a giant, running from a king trying to kill you, adultery, murder, war, a dysfunctional family, rape, and an attempted coup. Yup, all the elements.

You were definitely the original renaissance man: warrior, shepherd, and musician. And according to the Book, you were quite handsome too. You probably could have been on the cover of *People* magazine as the sexiest man alive, but being the humble man that you were, you probably turned it down.

Now about that meeting with Goliath. He was literally a giant, tall enough to be the starting center for any NBA team. He taunted you, and you weren't even quaking in your boots. Nope, you just took a rock, aimed it at him, and hit him smack-dab in the forehead, killing him dead.

You'd think King Saul would have been appreciative of how you whacked Goliath. But no, he got all jealous of your success and put a hit out on you. That had to be a rather sticky situation for you because you and the king's son were besties. And boy, oh boy, Saul tried to kill you more times than the coyote tried to catch the road runner.

But when you had a chance to take him out, you didn't. There he was, turning the cave into his personal porta potty, and you could have dusted him right then and there. But what did you do? You took out your scissors and snipped a piece of his robe. You were determined not to harm a hair on the head of the one the Lord had chosen, even though he deserved it. Did I just say that last part out loud here in heaven? And when you heard Saul had fallen on his sword in a battle with the Philistines, you mourned him and your beloved friend Jonathan. Then you became king, and there was still some drama there for those who were still #TeamSaul, even though he was very dead.

Now, let's talk about Bathsheba. This part of the story of your life played out like an episode of *General Hospital*. One lovely spring day when you should have been off to war, you were instead taking a stroll on the roof of your palace. That was when you noticed a young lovely taking a bath, and you sent for her. And then you two … well you know, 'cause later she sent you the message that there was a plus sign. She was pregnant and married, but not to you obviously.

Then you came up with quite the scheme. You called her husband back from the war, hoping he'd sleep with her and y'all could just say the baby was his. Your little plan could have worked, except her husband, Uriah, was a good soldier. He didn't feel right enjoying himself when his brethren were out there fighting the fight.

Then you had to come up with plan B, and it was a doozy. You wrote a letter to General Joab and had Uriah deliver it. The letter said to put Uriah on the front lines. So Uriah delivered the letter, which had instructions as to how he should be killed. Dang, that's cold. And side note, that's another example of why I don't understand people who say the Bible is boring. But back to you and your scheming. Sure enough, the general followed your orders and put Uriah on the frontlines, and he became a war casualty, killed in action.

Meanwhile back at the palace, after a respectable period of mourning, Bathsheba moved in, you two got hitched, and she had the baby. However, it was no surprise that the Lord was not pleased with your action. He sent Nathan the prophet to confront you and call you out. You finally confessed, but there were serious consequences for your actions. The baby got sick and died. But in your regret and grief, you didn't turn away from God. I guess that's why He blessed you with another son, Solomon.

There's so much more we could talk about, like how one of your sons rebelled against you and wanted you dead so he could take the throne. I'll save that for another day. But before I go, I do have a question for you: That time when you were dancing before the Lord—you know, the time you pretty much danced out of your clothes—you were doing the Electric Slide, right?

The David story:

1 Samuel 16–1 Kings 2

Deborah

Your Honor, it's a pleasure to meet you. So you were the only female judge mentioned in the Bible. You go, trailblazer! And you held court outside, under a palm tree. I know you didn't care about stuff like this, but you do know *The People's Court* would have given you much nicer digs, right?

Your CV must have been at least ten pages long: judge, warrior, poet, prophet, singer, songwriter. And to top it off, I read where you were described as a worshipping warrior. Those are some impressive credentials, Judge Deborah. I particularly love how you considered Israel as your children, even when they were acting wayward and misbehaving.

And the fact that you could hear from God—like, really hear from God—made all the difference. The best example was when Sisera, that ruthless commander of the Canaanite army, had been tormenting the people of Israel for twenty years. You called in Israel's own warrior, Barak, and gave him a battle plan straight from the Lord Himself. General Barak was to take ten thousand troops up to Mount Tabor, the Lord would make sure Sisera was lured to the right spot, and then General B could go in for the kill. Sounds like a simple enough plan to me, especially because God gave him the promise of victory. But what did Barak do? He said he wasn't going unless you went with him. Was he just being a chicken, or was something else at play here?

You told him you would go, but you warned that when the story came out in the paper the next day, the headline would be, "Woman

Captures and Conquers Sisera." And that was exactly what happened. It was quite a dramatic ending for his demise. When it was clear that Sisera's men were going to lose the battle, he ran away. What kind of general does that? And he ended up in the tent of Jael, who at first appeared to be quite the hostess. She gave him some milk (probably almond, no sugar added) and covered him with a nice fluffy rug (probably hot pink), and then just as he was getting relaxed and cozy, she took a hammer and drove a tent peg right into his temple. Ouch. That had to hurt.

So yup, all that you said came true. But I do have this question: Did a part of you want to look at Barak and say, "I don't need to say I told you so"?

The Deborah story:

Judges 4–5

Dorcas

Excuse me, hi, Dorcas. I just wanted to meet you. Or should I call you Tabitha? I loved reading your story because the first thing mentioned is how you were always doing good and being so charitable. I bet all the nonprofits in Joppa honored you with Citizen of the Year and a bunch of other community service awards. And they were all probably asking you to sit on their boards too, right? Did you?

I'm sure the community was so worried when you got sick and then devastated when you died. I just know everybody's timeline was flooded with, "RIH Dorcas." But then a miracle happened. When you were stretched out in the upper room (unlike Lazarus, they hadn't buried you at this point), the disciples sent two bike messengers to Peter, who was in nearby Lydda. The message was pretty direct: Get here yesterday.

Peter arrived on the scene and found the widows from the community there with your body, and they were distraught. They were showing him all the beautiful clothes you had made for them. My mom was a seamstress while I was growing up, by the way. See? We have something in common. But back to you being dead and all. Peter politely asked everyone to leave the room, kneeled down, prayed, and then turned to your body and said, "Tabitha, arise." He called you by your Aramaic name, which apparently you recognized because you opened your eyes, saw Peter, and sat up.

What a commotion that must have caused when your widow friends saw their community champion was alive and well. But here's a question for you: Everywhere you went from then on, did people stare and whisper, "There's the lady who was temporarily dead. Let's take a selfie with her"?

The Dorcas/Tabitha story:

Acts 9:36–43

Enoch

Well, hello there, Enoch. I guess you've been here for quite some time.

Your story in the Book is short—very short, in fact—but it sure is major. You are the father of the oldest man to ever live on planet Earth, Methuselah. Congratulations on that. But your story, wow! You were walking around one day, and God took you. You disappeared. One minute you were there, and the next you were gone. Just like that. The great disappearing act. You're even mentioned in Hebrews 11, the Hall of Faith. God said you trusted Him, and He was pleased with you and took you away. Dude! You didn't die! How amazing is that? You were just walking along your merry way, probably walking to the mailbox or something, and thinking about what a beautiful day it was. Then, poof—there you were with God.

I'm honored to meet you. But I do have a question for you: Did they put up missing posters about you?

Enoch's story:

Genesis 5:18–24

Esther

With all due respect to Aretha, Latifah, and even Elizabeth, you, Esther, are *the* queen, the OG of all queens.

Your story would have made for great reality TV, number one on Netflix guaranteed. Let's face it. It's the story of a young girl orphaned and taken in by her cousin, who raised her like a daughter. She grew up to be a lovely young woman, lovely enough to be in the pageant for … the next queen of Ancient Persia.

And let me say you handled that process like a boss. Twelve months of being beautified with cosmetics and perfumes and oils and whatnot, even though I'm sure you were already ultralovely and didn't need all that extra stuff. So I'm curious about the details that aren't mentioned in your story. Like, did you see the other young women before they went to meet the king? And more important, did you see them when they returned? Were y'all sizing each other up and comparing notes? I'm quite curious.

Moving right along, obviously you dazzled Your Majesty because he took one look at you and put the crown right on your head. Did they sing, "There she is, Queeeen Eeeesther"?

Oh, but royal life was not carefree for you, was it? Cousin Mordecai told you not to reveal you were Jewish. But when that scoundrel Haman put out a contract on the Jews, Mordecai challenged you to plead with the king to save your people. I like how you gave the safe response at first: "Listen, cuz. Everybody knows that if you go to the king without being summoned, you might get whacked." I'll be honest, that's probably what I would have said at first too.

And that was when Cousin Mordecai had to break it down. The palace walls would not be high enough or strong enough to protect you from being wiped out with the rest of your people. And then you did a total boss move, told everybody to fast, and said these words that showed us how much courage you had. It's the words gospel great Albertina Walker sang back in the day: "If I perish, let me perish. I'm going to see the King." You did, and you saved your people. Let me say it one more time: total boss.

But I do have one more question for you: You had to wait an entire year to be presented to the king. When you first saw him, were you thinking, "I'd like to cancel this episode of *Married at First Sight*"?

Esther's story:

Esther

Eve

Guuurrrl. You know we blamed you for a lot. Yes, I know, kinda self-righteous of us, thinking we would not have been fooled in that situation.

I kinda felt sorry for you though. It must have been so hard to carry around all that guilt and regret, thinking about what you did and how your life would be so different if you had just listened to God instead of that crafty serpent. You can't trust snakes. I've known that all my life.

And I'm guessing your heart was beating a million miles a minute when God was looking for you, and you and Adam were trying to hide—you know, feeling all guilty and realizing you'd been walking around happy and naked, until your encounter with the deceiver.

Oh, and another thing: I'm really sorry about Abel. Your heart had to break, knowing your son killed your other son. That was a lot for any parent to bear on Earth. I have a question for you: On the way out of the Garden, did Adam look at you and say, "I told you not to talk to strangers"?

Eve's story:

Genesis 2–3

Gideon

Hello there, Gideon. I'll resist the urge to say, "Where you been hiding?" 'cause that would be totally corny, right?

It's nice to see you because I want to let you know I admire your courage. Yes, courage. I know that might sound strange because when we're introduced to you, you are anything but courageous. And your self-esteem? Well, let's face it: it's lower than low. After all, when the Angel paid you a visit and addressed you as a mighty man of valor, you were like, "Ahh, Mr. Angel, I think you have the wrong address." In fact, you went so far as to inform him that not only was your family not a member of high society in the tribe of Manasseh, but you were the lowest of the low in your own family. Serious self-esteem issues, dude.

But I do admire the fact that you were brave enough to ask for proof on several occasions. I mean, fire had to come out of a rock before you were convinced the angel's message was the real deal.

You had the courage to tear down your father's altar of Baal (at night, though, because you were scared of your father and some of those "menfolk" in town).

And what about your test of the fleece? Pretty bold of you to ask for a sign the first time, but then to ask for a second test? Yup, kinda bold.

Then there was the time when you were getting ready to go into battle against the Midianites, and God thinned the ranks down to three hundred soldiers. Your confidence was boosted when you overheard a conversation about a dream where you were victorious. And let's just say when you went to battle, you were all in.

But I do have this one question: When God kept telling you that you had too many soldiers for battle, were you thinking that God's not good at math?

Gideon's story:

Judges 6–8

Hannah

Don't tell the others, but you were one of my favorites. Honestly. In fact, besides the Bible, I read another book about you because I was always so fascinated by how you waited and prayed and never gave up. And girl, you had some patience!

So let's talk about that bully, your rival, the original mean girl, Peninnah, tormenting you because she had a slew of kids and you couldn't get pregnant. She made you cry and made you so sad that you couldn't eat.

But still you didn't clap back. How did you do that? How could you stand being in the same house with that … ah, because we're in heaven, I'll say woman. But just between us girls, you did at least give her the eyeroll, right?

Now, I must tell you, I've gone back and forth on how I feel about your hubby, Elkanah. I know he was all about trying to make you not feel bad about the way Peninnah treated you. He made sure you got extra gifts and all that, and obviously you were the favorite wife. However, I wanted him to put P in her place on more than one occasion.

Nevertheless, you persisted!

Yup, you kept praying. And that time when Eli thought you were drunk at church, you were actually pouring your heart out to God and promising that if He'd give you a son, you'd give him back. Whoa! That's a huge promise.

Obviously He heard you because you got pregnant and welcomed bouncing baby boy Samuel into the world. I'm assuming that Peninnah did not throw you a baby shower.

Then you followed through on what you said. You brought Samuel back to the temple, back to God. That must have been a tough conversation: "Son, I prayed for you so long, I love you so much, but I'm leaving you here at the Temple." But God really honored you after that, didn't He? You went on to have three more sons and two daughters.

Take that, Peninnah!

I do have one question: Did you secretly wish, even a little bit, that Peninnah would stub her toe, get tennis elbow, or at least an itchy weird rash?

Hannah's story:

1 Samuel 1–2

Isaac

Isaac, hi! Okay, first of all, go ahead and admit it. They totally spoiled you, didn't they? Your parents, Abraham and Sarah, waited forever and a day to have a child (as in a child together, but we won't get into that other entanglement right now), so it's understandable that you may have been just a little spoiled.

However, remember that time your dad was going to kill you? Of course you remember. But I've always wondered what you were thinking. Y'all were on a boys' trip—you, your dad, and a couple of servants. Your father stopped to build an altar. Everything was cool so far, but then he tied you up and laid you on the altar over the wood. I'd like to know what you were doing at that very moment. Were you squirming? Were your armpits a little sweaty? You did ask the obvious question, "Hey, Dad, we have the wood and flint to make the fire, but where is the lamb?" But the big question is did you resist, or did you simply stand there and let him tie you up and lay you on that pile of wood? Inquiring minds want to know.

But just as he raised the knife and was about to gut you like a fish, God called out and told him to slow his roll. Whew! And behold, there was a ram in the bush, and you were spared.

Okay, now let's move along to talk about your life with your wife, Rebekah, and the twins, Esau and Jacob. Rebekah and Jacob did you dirty. Taking advantage of an elderly blind man is pretty low. They tricked you into giving the blessing to Jacob instead of Esau, the oldest twin. And all you and Esau could do was weep.

Anyway, my question for you: That time when you and your dad returned from the trip where he almost took you out, when you got home, did you tell Sarah what happened when she asked how was your trip? Something like, "Well, Mom, it was certainly interesting. Dad was gonna kill me, but God intervened. What's for dinner?"

Isaac's story:

Genesis 21–28

Jacob

Hi, Jacob. Well, you turned out to be quite the character study. First, you have the distinction of being the first twin recorded in the Bible—you and your brother Esau. And what a relationship the two of you had. I guess we shouldn't be surprised because you were born holding your brother's heel. You were trying to come out first, weren't you?

I know you're glad to be here. No more being weighed down with the label of being the deceiver, the trickster, the supplanter. That scheme you and your mother, Rebekah, cooked up to deceive your father was really something. You dressed up like your brother, brought Dad some of his favorite food, and fooled your old, practically blind father into blessing you instead of Esau. And Esau was none too happy and intended to kill you once your father was dead and buried. So you did the only sensible thing: you headed for the hills and ended up at your Uncle Laban's house.

One day, Uncle Laban came to you with a proposal. He'd pay you for your hard work. You had fallen in love with his stunning daughter Rachel, so you agreed to work seven years for her hand in marriage. When the seven years were up, Laban threw a big wedding. But the reception must have been quite lively, because the next morning, you woke up not to Rachel but to her slightly less attractive older sister, Leah. Yup, the playa got played! You had to spend what I'm sure felt like a very long week with Leah, and then you got Rachel after agreeing to work another seven years.

At some point, Laban and his sons started having some serious attitude toward you, so you decided to head back home. On the journey there, you had a wrestling match with God. You came away with your hip out of socket, a blessing, and a new name, Israel. Eventually you even had a reunion with your brother, Esau. It was not what you expected. He ran to you and threw his arms around you, and you both got weepy. Maybe those gifts you sent ahead for him softened his heart. We really saw how God worked through you, flaws and all.

I have a question for you before I go: If cameras had been rolling the morning you woke up and discovered you'd spent your wedding night with Leah and not Rachel, would we have needed to bleep the first words you said?

More on Jacob:

Genesis 25:19–34
Genesis 27–35

Job

Finally! I've been looking everywhere for you. I didn't give up though. I had the patience of … well, you know. I know, I know, you've probably heard that one million times by now. You gotta admit, it is at least kinda funny, right?

I know we just met, and please don't be offended, but I feel the need to say your friends were the worst. Yes, I will give them credit for coming to see you in your time of need and for sitting there and just being with you in their silence for seven days. But when they finally started talking, that was when things went south.

Let's back up and talk about your pretrouble days, when you were ballin'. You had a lot of land and livestock, probably a big tent mansion, and the latest fleet of camels; made the cover of *Rich Uz Living* magazine every year, and had all the things that signaled you were financially set.

Life was good until satan thought he could break you. You know that song from the musical *The Wiz*, "Don't Nobody Bring Me No Bad News"? That could have been your theme song. In one day, you lost your livestock, servants, and your mode of transportation, and just when it looked like things couldn't get any worse, your sons and daughters were killed in a powerful desert windstorm. And after that? Yup, the hits kept on coming because you broke out in some nasty sores from head to toe. By that time, wifey had had enough and told you to curse God and die. But you didn't. You held on.

Now, at this point, the three stooges, your three friends, arrived on the scene. Like I said earlier, it started out great until they started speaking and blaming you for all your troubles, trying to get you to admit to some sin and repent. With friends like that …!

However, you rather eloquently defended yourself to all three of them. My favorite part is that you told them that when it comes to comforting, they were pretty much terrible.

Then you and God had a come to Jesus moment. He reminded you of who He is and what He can do. And after everything you went through, God restored you with health and strength, more children, and thousands of sheep, camels, oxen, and donkeys.

I do have one question: After those three friends left with their bad advice, did they check on you again, or did you ghost 'em?

The Job story:

Job

John the Apostle

Good evening, John. Not quite sure how to address you because you have quite a few names: John the Apostle, St. John, John of Patmos, and John the Revelator. Still, for a lot of my earlier years, I thought you and John the Baptist were the same person. My apologies. I like the Revelator the best, so can I just call you JTR? I can? Okay, thanks.

It must have been quite an experience being in Jesus's inner circle. In John, your book, you wrote that you were the disciple whom Jesus loved. He even gave you and your brother James nicknames, Sons of Thunder. That's a pretty cool nickname. I'm wondering if that refers to your personalities. After all, that time when a group of Samaritans so rudely didn't welcome Jesus into the village, you and your brother asked Him if He wanted you to call down fire from heaven and destroy them. I bet you and your brother were just itching to do that. But Jesus didn't sign off on it. You can go ahead and tell me: You were disappointed, weren't you?

To think it all started when you and your brother were with your dad working on the nets at the family fishing business, and along came Jesus with a simple invitation: "Follow Me." And you did, both of you. And what a journey you had, being there for the major moments in Jesus's life, like the Mount of Transfiguration when Jesus was chatting it up with Moses and Elijah. He even took you with Him to the Garden of Gethsemane. By the way, you must have been really exhausted because he told you to watch and pray, but when He came back, you were snoring. You, your brother, and Peter obviously forgot to put No Doze and a Red Bull in your backpack.

What's so beautiful is that at the crucifixion, Jesus trusted you enough that He asked you to look after his precious mother, Mary.

Here's where your life took a dramatic turn. All the preaching, teaching, and talking about Jesus got you exiled and imprisoned on the island of Patmos. I know prison isn't supposed to be a plush hotel, but it was even worse for you—you were living in a cave. However, it was there in those dire conditions where the Holy Spirit gave you the book of Revelation. So you commenced to writing about stuff you were seeing a gazillion years into the future. And you wrote it by hand. Did you get writer's cramp? You probably would have won the National Book Review grand prize, but some of the stuff you wrote scared us, some of it totally confused us, and some of it we didn't fully understand until we got here. Now, I understand that you didn't know what some of the stuff was because it was so far into the future. You were simply fulfilling your mission to write what you saw.

Well, you do have the distinction of being the apostle who died at a ripe old age. But I have a question from your younger days: When Jesus called you and your brother, and you immediately left what you were doing, was your dad cool with that, or did he say, "Where y'all going? Come back here and help me with these nets"?

John's writings:

John
1 John
2 John
3 John
Revelation

John the Baptist

Hey! Good afternoon! I've been looking for you. There's so much cool stuff about your story. First of all, we see the great mission you had before you were even born. Luke said you would be great in the sight of the Lord, you'd be filled with the Holy Spirit while still in the womb, and you'd be a forerunner of Christ—lots of cool things.

Your parents, Zechariah and Elizabeth (I can't wait to meet them too, by the way), had waited for you a long time—so long that when the angel Gabriel told your daddy you were on the way, he expressed some doubt and ended up not being able to speak until you were born. By the way, that was really a sweet moment when Mary came to visit, and you heard her voice and leaped for joy, like you were saying, "Hey cuz, from in here." I can imagine all the townsfolks were quite surprised when they expected you to be named Zechariah Jr., but your father connected to Wi-Fi and wrote on his tablet, "His name is John."

You know the old saying "You can't judge a book by its cover"? That was totally you. I mean, let's talk about your wardrobe. Camel hair and leather—you know those two don't go together, right? Your diet of locusts and wild honey sounds a little out there as well. And I'll bet you a box of cupcakes that you had crazy, wild hair. Then to top it off, you were living in the woods. I mean, the society folks in Judea must have thought you were totally weird. But you could have won *Survivor* hands down.

It didn't really matter what they thought. You continued your mission of preaching, preparing the way, and then even though you meant it when you said, "I'm not worthy," you went on to be the one who baptized Jesus Christ Himself.

I truly admire your courage to speak out, even when it cost you everything, as in your life and your head—your actual head. I'm talking about when you boldly told King Herod that it was wrong for him to marry his brother's wife, Herodias. Then at his birthday bash, Herodias's daughter did some *Dancing with the Stars* moves and got perfect scores from Herod, so he agreed to give her anything she wanted. After conferring with her mother, she asked for your head on a platter, and that was what she got. And looking at you now, let me just say I'm glad for the promise of new, heavenly bodies.

But I do have one question: Are locusts keto?

More about John the Baptist:

Matthew 3
Mark 1:1–15
Luke 1
Matthew 14: 1-12

Jonah

Well, hello there, Jonah. So you really thought you could run away from the Lord's assignment? He told you to go to the big city of Ninevah and preach against it and its wicked ways. You instead decided to get out of Dodge and head to Tarshish.

So you high-tailed it to Joppa, paid your fare, and hopped aboard a ship, destination Tarshish—or so you thought. I guess you were in such a big hurry that you didn't take time to check the weather report, because the Doppler radar would have clearly shown there was a big storm approaching.

Being on the lam from the Lord must have been rather tiring because when your shipmates were freaking out about the storm, you were below deck in a deep sleep, probably snoring as loud as the wind.

I think the sailors do deserve a little credit for not immediately throwing you overboard when they cast lots and discovered you brought all the trouble aboard. But when they couldn't take it anymore, yup, they tossed you overboard, and the big fish caught you. There you were in the belly of the fish for three long days and nights. After the initial terror, that must have been really boring in those first few hours. No Hulu, no gaming devices, and not even a deck of cards. Oh, but you had plenty of time to pray and think about what the Lord told you to do. So when the big fish had a little case of acid reflux, it spit you out on the beach.

This time, you understood the assignment, followed the bright lights to Ninevah, and commenced to preaching. The people listened and turned their lives around. Wait, what? Yup, they actually listened to you and obeyed. Sounds like a great end to your story. But nooo, you actually had the nerve to get mad that God relented and didn't destroy them. You realize how crazy that sounds right now, correct? The Lord had to set you straight on that, and He did.

I do have this question: You probably never ate another fish sandwich after that, huh?

Jonah's story:

Jonah

Joseph (Old Testament)

Joseph! Hey! Your story would have made for a great true-crime podcast. There's jealousy in the family, a kidnapping, being falsely accused of a crime, languishing in prison until you are finally released, and then a dramatic reunion with your brothers who betrayed you.

So knowing you were your father's favorite, please tell me what possessed you to tell your brothers about your dreams—the dreams where you were the boss of them?

I'm not saying it was right what they did to you in their jealousy, tossing you in a pit, selling you for twenty pieces of silver, and lying to your father that some wild, vicious animal had eaten you for brunch. Nope, nothing right about that. But your big mouth—pardon me, I mean your gregarious nature taught us about not sharing our dreams with everybody.

Moving right along to the time when you were Potiphar's personal assistant and house manager, which was some more serious drama. Your boss's wife liked what she saw and tried to seduce you. You get the Willpower of the Century award when you told her that would be disrespectful to your boss and a great evil and sin against God.

However, after turning her down more than once, Mrs. Potiphar claimed you tried to rape her, so Potiphar believed her lies and sent you straight to jail. Do not pass go. Do not collect two hundred dollars.

And here's what's so cool: Even in the clink, God was granting you favor with the warden. You probably got a little extra dessert at dinner, and they made sure you had a few shekels on your prison books.

I suppose you got a little frustrated, though, when you interpreted a dream for your prison mate, the king's cupbearer, and he said he'd tell Pharoah what you'd done. Yet once he was free, he forgot all about you, until two years later when Pharoah had another dream that needed interpreting. That turned out to be your "get out of jail free" card.

So you went from the pit to the palace, this time as the vice president of Egypt, getting everything ready for the seven years of prosperity and seven years of famine. Everything was finally going well for you, and you even got a wife. Congratulations! How was the wedding?

But during the famine, look who showed up at the palace looking to buy some grain, because the shelves at the Sam's Club of Canaan were stripped bare. Yup, your brothers! They didn't recognize you, but you certainly recognized them. I guess it's hard to forget the people who sold you. I like how you waited for a few days and put a few tests before them before you finally revealed your identity.

And here's the best part: you were reunited with your father, Israel/ Jacob. That must have been quite a sight with no dry eye in the house.

I have a question for you: Is the coat of many colors here? Can I see it?

Joseph's story:

Genesis 37–50

Joseph (New Testament)

Okay, I'm having a total fangirl moment right now. Let me say that we didn't give you nearly enough credit. I know you don't care about stuff like that, but I feel like we totally underplayed just how important you were in the Jesus story. I mean, you set a whole new standard for bonus fathers.

I've wondered how you really felt when Mary told you she was pregnant. I'm guessing you were excited about the upcoming marriage, and you probably had a whole little life plan in mind. You'd get married, get a nice little house in the burbs in Nazareth, run your carpentry business, and raise a family, and Mary would be a stay-at-home mom. Then she upped and told you she was pregnant, and the father was … wait for it … God! That had to leave your head spinning.

How did you explain that to your family and your boys, who had to be looking at you like, "Right, Joe. Your girl is pregnant, and you are not the father!" They probably asked if you were planning a DNA test.

But this is what I mean about how honorable you were. You were going to quietly break off the relationship until the angel appeared and told you, "Yup, it's true. Mary conceived by way of the Holy Spirit Himself." Then you were fully onboard with the plan.

And the whole no room in the inn thing? You didn't even go off on all the innkeepers who turned you away. You weren't tempted to say, "Look, man, don't you know who I am? I'm about to be raising the Son of God!" They probably wouldn't have believed you anyway.

Oh, and that time when Jesus was twelve, y'all took him to the temple in Jerusalem, and on the way back home, you realized you'd left him behind? God was looking out for you because nobody called the Galilee Department of Children and Families.

I bring that up because that's the last we heard of you. What happened to you?

Well, I just want you to know that I recognize the significant part you played in our salvation story. You protected Mary, you protected Jesus, and you were a man of great faith.

I do have this question: Jesus was perfect. He was fully God but also fully man. So as a little boy, did Jesus ever get put in time out?

Joseph's story:

Luke 1–2
Matthew 1–2

Joshua

Joshua! It's an honor to see you in person. You were quite the warrior, field general, and spy all rolled into one.

You could have been in the CIA. Moses sent you, Caleb, and ten other spies to scout out Canaan, the land the Lord promised to you Israelites. The others came back with their scaredy-cat reports about how well the city was protected, how the people there were so big and strong, blah, blah, blah. But you and Caleb were like, "We got this." And it didn't work out so well for the nervous nellies because they all died when the plague came.

Anyway, let's move along to the Battle of Jericho. That was so impressive that we wrote a song about it. Wanna hear it? Here it goes: "Joshua fit the battle of Jericho, and the walls came tumbling down." This is pretty cool. I've discovered here in heaven, I can actually sing. Okay, back to your story. I bet when God told you what to do, you were thinking, "What kind of crazy battle plan is that?" Let's see, march around the city once. Got it. Do that for six days. Got it. On day seven, march around the city seven times, have the priests blow the trumpets, and then everybody shout at the top of their lungs, and the city walls will collapse.

What did you tell the reporters at the news conference when they asked you about your battle plan? "General Joshua, did I hear you correctly? You're going to march around the city for a week, and you expect the walls to just fall down?" Weirdest battle plan in the history of battles. But it worked, and you were the hero of the day!

I have this one question: I know you're a confident but humble man, but when the walls came tumbling down, did you crack a slight smile and say under your breath, "That went well"?

Joshua's story:

Numbers 13
Deuteronomy 31
Joshua

Lazarus

Pleased to meet you. You would have made a great question on *Jeopardy*: He's the only person who died and was buried twice and will live in eternity. Who is Lazarus?

You and Jesus were friends—not just acquaintances but real friends. John said Jesus loved you and your sisters, Martha and Mary. He probably came over to the house for a barbecue, watched a little football, and had some sweet tea—that sorta friend. So I guess when you got sick, you didn't panic. You didn't need Bethany's top doc because you had a direct line to Dr. Jesus. Well, I imagine you were quite surprised when you kept getting worse, and your pal Jesus still hadn't shown up. And here's the killing part (no pun intended): He knew you were sick! Somebody told Him, emailed Him, tagged Him on social media, or something, so He knew. And then you died … that must have been weird.

When He did show up, you'd already been physically cooling your heels (again, no pun intended) for four long days. All the family, friends, and folks from the town were gathering, crying, and consoling each other. Jesus was clearly touched and started crying. See? He really did love you. Oh, and by the way, there were some petty Pattys in town who were saying, "If this joker could heal the blind, why couldn't He heal you?" They spoke too soon.

While all this commotion was going on, I guess all of a sudden, you heard your friend calling your name and calling you to come out of the tomb. So out you walked, with your hands and feet bound in linen, looking like the original mummy. Everybody there witnessed a truly great miracle. That must have been quite a sight. And it must have been quite a reunion and celebration.

I have a question: When you walked out of the tomb, did you look at Jesus and say, "Yo, dude, what took you so long?"

The Lazarus story:

John 11

Luke

Hello, Luke—oh, excuse me, Dr. Luke.

Well, I guess we could consider you the first and original president of the American Medical Association. What's it like being here where you have no patients—zero, not a single one—because nobody is sick here? That's just glorious, wouldn't you say?

You and Paul were kinda like best buds, and you were with Jesus on several missionary journeys. I suppose that's why you wrote a lot of the New Testament—more than 25 percent with your books, Luke and Acts. Good thing those Google docs automatically save themselves, right?

I'd like to say thank you for your attention to detail. You're really the one who gave us the deets on the Christmas story, the Beatitudes, and the Transfiguration, to name a few. You included many stories about Jesus's healing ministry. Of course you did, because you were a doctor. I see what you did there. It certainly worked out for Paul to have his own concierge medical doctor because he got a beatdown more than once for spreading the Gospel.

It's rather interesting that you wrote so much, but you're only mentioned by name a few times in the whole Bible. We don't know much about your background or your family. But we do know you were serious about your writings for us, were a loyal friend, and stayed with Paul until the end.

I have a question for you, Dr. Luke: Did Paul ever get a bill for all the times you treated him?

Luke's writings:

Luke
Acts

Lydia

Hi, Lydia. I knew that was you; I recognized your beautiful purple outfit.

Yours was another one of those stories that was short but extremely impactful. After all, you are considered the first person converted in Europe.

It sounds like you had quite an interesting life, growing up in the ritzy city of Thyatira. You were obviously an excellent businesswoman with a thriving company selling purple cloth, because only the well-heeled people wore purple. I bet you won the Chamber's Business of the Year award more than once. Congratulations.

But here's where your life took a dramatic turn. It was that day you and some of the women in your small group gathered by a river in Philippi to have a prayer meeting. That was where Paul and his fellow missionaries saw you. Paul shared his message of the Gospel, and you accepted Jesus and got baptized right then and there. And that's not all. Everybody in your household accepted Jesus and got baptized too. Clearly you were not messing around.

Then you showed us just how generous you were with your wealth when you invited Paul and his crew to stay at your house! That's a lesson in Hospitality 101.

I do have a question for you: You were with a group of women praying, and a group of men approached you. At first, did you give them a look that said, "This isn't the club, and we're not interested in you. Now, hit the bricks"?

Lydia's story:

Acts 16

Mark

Hi! Do you like to be called John Mark or just Mark? I know you probably got tired of everybody treating you like a kid, but it must have been quite an experience being young and growing up in the early Church. Were you active in the youth group? Did you sing in the young choir and serve on the junior usher board?

Of all the writers of the Gospels, we know the least about you. Was that by design? Whatever the case, I'm here to give you props because I like your writing style. Your book is succinct and straight to the point. And you seemed to be targeting the Gentiles with your message. Thanks for that.

Things seemed to be going well for you when you tagged along with your cuz Barnabus and Paul on that first missionary journey. Apparently at some point, you bailed out on them and Ubered back to Jerusalem. But you didn't tell us why, and I'm quite curious. Somebody had a beef? Then on the second missionary journey, Barnabus wanted you to join them. Paul nixed that idea. So with blood being thicker than water, Barnabus left Paul, and you and your cousin B hopped a sailboat to Cyprus. Fortunately, y'all didn't all stay mad at each other forever. You reconciled, because later on, Paul described you as being useful to him in ministry.

Before I go, I'd like to ask you a question: When you wrote about the night Jesus was arrested, you mentioned that a young man wearing a linen cloth was in the crowd of onlookers, and some in the mob tried to grab him. When he was trying to get away, his cloth came off, and he ran away in his birthday suit, naked. That was you, wasn't it?

Mark's writings:

Mark

Martha

I'm thrilled to meet you. You know, in the Christian community, we were often asked if we were a Martha or a Mary. I think we all wanted to be able to say we were a Mary, but I'll confess that a lot of time I was you, a Martha, so busy doing stuff that I didn't take enough time to sit and be in the presence of Jesus.

I get why you were so concerned with making sure everything was perfect when Jesus arrived for dinner at your house. You were the hostess with the mostest, with the kind of social skills that would make Miss Manners proud. I'm guessing you were laying out a fancy charcuterie board, watching over appetizers in the air fryer, and checking up on something tasty in the slow cooker. That all takes some time, and you can't very well serve the King of Kings something from the Bethany Burger King.

We don't want to admit it, but we also would be a little put off by doing all the work while our sister is chillaxing with the guest of honor, even when it's Jesus Himself.

I really want to know what you were thinking when Lazarus got sick, and you and Mary called for Jesus to come to him. Y'all were like the Fab Four, but Jesus seemed to take his sweet time to get there. When He finally arrived, Lazarus was already dead and laid in his tomb. I'd like to know your tone when you ran to meet Jesus. Were you speaking to him out of your heartbreak and tears, or just between us girls, were you a little salty that he got there late? You know, something like,

"You are our friend. We needed You. If You had gotten here on time like we asked, our brother wouldn't be dead right now."

But after Jesus reminded you about the promise of the resurrection, everything—and I mean everything—changed at the cemetery. I like how you tried to warn Him the smell would be kinda ripe because Laz had been dead for four days.

You were there front and center, an eyewitness to one of the greatest miracles of all time, when Jesus called your brother forth, and he walked out of the tomb, still wrapped in his funeral attire but pretty much fresh as a daisy. That was a scene worthy of breaking news and the lead on the six o'clock news.

I do have this question: Did Lazarus ask any obvious questions, like, "So, sisters, anything exciting happen during the four days while I was dead?"

Martha's story:

Luke 10:38–42
John 11:1–44

Mary

Mary, did you know? I've been waiting a lifetime to say that to you. I know you've probably heard it before, but thanks for smiling and making me feel like I'm original and this is the first time anyone has said that to you. That song about you is really beautiful. I'm sure you like it too.

I hope you made your plans in pencil because God definitely had the eraser when it came to your life. There you were, planning your wedding. You were excited about marrying Joseph and building a nice, comfortable life with him. Obviously he'd be building the house, with him being a carpenter and all. Sounds like a good life plan for a nice young lady like you in Nazareth.

But then, whoa! Pump the brakes! The angel Gabriel stopped by to deliver some change your life news to you. You are going to get pregnant, but not in the traditional way. The Holy Spirit would come upon you. I can imagine you were having one of those "What the what?" moments. But that was not all. The baby you were going to have would be … are you ready? The Son of God. After the initial shock, you were like, "Okay, count me in."

Then you had to tell everyone, including your family and Joseph. How did you start that conversation? "So, Joseph, you know how we're waiting until we get married? Well, I'm pregnant." I'm sure you were the talk of all the gossipers in Galilee. But when Joseph believed the angel, that must have made you love him even more. Cue the violins because that had the makings of a Hallmark movie.

Now, about the birth of Jesus. There was no hospital with a fancy birthing center. The Bethlehem Ritz was all booked, so you ended up in a stable giving birth to sweet baby Jesus. Nowhere is it recorded that you ever complained about the accommodations. You could have said, "Excuse me, Mr. Concierge. I know you said the hotel is booked, but I'm about to give birth to God's Son. So I'm pretty sure you can find a VIP suite, a regular suite, or at least a room with a king-sized bed for *the* King." But no, you were humble and simply went along with God's plan.

Did I mention I admire everything about you? I think you would have won Mom of the Year hands down, every single year.

It must have been an experience watching Jesus grow up, begin His ministry, and take on the sins of the world at Calvary. And He made sure He left someone to look after you.

There's so much I could say about you. Your life was simply extraordinary. But I do have this question: When Jesus turned water into wine at the fancy wedding in Cana, did the other guests ask you if He'd come to their house and do that too?

Mary's story:

Matthew 1–2
Luke 1–2
John 2:1–12

Mary Magdalene

Good morning, Mary! This place sure is a lot different from Magdala, wouldn't you say? People throughout the ages certainly had a lot to say about you. Isn't it wonderful to be here where we all see you for who you really are?

Your social media profile is amazing: Christ follower, delivered from demons, eyewitness to the most important events in Christianity, Magdala's most well-known resident.

We didn't get details about how long you had been tormented by demons, but your life changed radically when Jesus came along and cast them out of you. And you became a devoted follower of Christ. You didn't need to be on an episode of *Iyanla, Fix My Life*—you had Jesus Himself.

I'm glad we have eternity here because I want to hear all about what it was like following Jesus, the people you met, places you visited—everything. And I know some of the things you saw broke your heart at the time. They could have done an entire episode about you on the old TV show *You Are There*, because you were. You were there when Christ was convicted in that kangaroo court. You were there when He got the death sentence; I'm guessing your heart sank at that moment. You were there when Jesus was beaten. And you were there when He was hanging on the cross in agony. It had to be devastating to stand there with His mother as well.

I imagine you were inconsolable that weekend after all you had seen. You probably stayed in bed crying, hoping you'd wake up from that nightmare. But that's not the end of His story, or yours. Very early that Sunday morning, you forced yourself to get out of bed. It was so early that it was still dark, but you and your two friends were on a mission to get to the tomb with spices. You got there, but wait ... what? The tomb ... it's empty. Jesus's body was not there!

This was where you should have won a Pulitzer Prize for reporting. You ran back and found Peter and another disciple and shouted this headline: "The tomb is empty."

Then y'all did your best Usain Bolt and raced back to the tomb. Update: it was still empty. Still no Jesus, just the linens from his burial outfit. As you were standing outside the tomb weeping because you thought somebody had made off with the corpse, two angels appeared and asked why you were crying. As you were answering them, Jesus appeared. But you didn't recognize Him and thought He was the gardener until He said your name, Mary. Cue the music. I can't even imagine how emotional that must have been for you.

But Jesus cut the reunion short because He had a message for you to deliver to the disciples. Yes, He trusted you that much. So off you went to the disciples with another headline: "I have seen the Lord."

I have one question: Weren't you a tiny bit worried somebody would ask, "What have you been smoking?" when you told them you'd seen a man who had been dead a few days ago but was now alive and well?

Mary Magdalene's story:

Matthew 28:1–10
Mark 15:40–47
Mark 16:1–11
Luke 24:1–11
John 19:23–27
John 20:1–18

Mary of Bethany

Hello, Mary. Just as I expected, you're just sitting around, chilling, resting, and relaxing. Too soon?

Seriously, so many of us were Marthas, with a goal of becoming more like you.

Lady, you had your priorities straight. Jesus came to your house to visit you, your sister Martha, and your brother Lazarus. I can just hear some of your jealous neighbors: "What's so special about them? And why don't they each have their own house, instead of all living together there?" Others were most likely saying, "What's all the fuss over this Jesus fella, anyway? He's walking around claiming to be the Son of God. We think He's crazy."

And while Martha was busy being super hostess, you were just sitting at the feet of Jesus, listening to Him. When your sis was being a tattletale and let Jesus know she was the one doing all the work, Jesus let her know you had chosen the right and best thing. Mary for the win!

Then when y'all texted Jesus to tell him his brother from another mother was sick, you expected Him to drop everything and take the express lane to Bethany. Martha was probably pacing the floor, looking out the window every five minutes. You were probably relaxing in the Lazy Boy, wearing out the remote control.

But then your beloved brother died. Jesus was a no-show. When He finally did get there, He was moved by the depth of your grief. But your mourning soon turned to dancing when Jesus called your brother out of the tomb fully alive, healthy, and not even smelling like death.

You continued to show your big ol' heart just days before the crucifixion. Jesus came back to visit, and you broke open that bottle of Chanel, poured it on the Son of God's feet, and wiped them with your hair. Of course Judas chimed in and complained that the perfume could have been sold and the money given to the poor. He was as crooked as the day is long, embezzling money from the treasury—just your basic thief. Fortunately, Jesus stepped in to defend you.

Yup, nothing but respect for you. I'm sure we'll chat again soon, but before you go, I have one question for you: Did you show Lazarus the funeral program after he was alive again?

Mary's story:

Luke 10:38–42
John 11:1–44
John 12:1–8

Matthew

Well, well, well, if it isn't Mr. IRS himself. I'm happy to see you, and I'm happy that we don't have to pay taxes here. You won't be offended if I bring up your past to talk about your transformation, will you?

You were a tax collector—not exactly a noble profession in those days. Y'all were notorious for lying about what people owed and then pocketing the difference. Totally unscrupulous. And you were a Jew working for the Roman government, so you were kind of a turncoat. In fact, you were sitting in your plush office in Capernaum, probably figuring out whom you were going to scam next and how you were going to avoid the local consumer reporter looking into citizen complaints against you. That was when Jesus called you to follow Him, and you became a part of Jesus's big twelve traveling crew.

What about the time you threw a dinner party at your huge mansion, and Jesus showed up to dine with your roster of sinner guests? The self-righteous Pharisees were of course beside themselves to see Jesus hanging out with such an unsavory crowd. But Jesus set 'em straight, letting them know it was the sick folks who needed a doctor, and that was why He came for them. Mic drop for Jesus on that one.

Despite your past, you became an eyewitness to the life of Jesus and recorded much of it for us in the book of Matthew, one of the four gospels. I know I've talked a lot about your past, but it's so important in how it shows us Jesus can use anyone and how He can completely transform lives. You walked away from a cushy job and a lavish lifestyle to follow Jesus. You traded earthly rewards for eternal ones. That's an important lesson for us all.

Before I go, a question for you: When you threw that big party at your palatial estate, did you say on the e-vite that Jesus was the guest of honor, or did people simply show up and say, "Who's that party crasher?"

Matthew's writings:

Matthew

Moses

Good evening, Moses! Your story certainly read like a Hollywood blockbuster, and I'm sure you know it was a movie. Did you like it?

It has all the compelling events: You were given up for adoption, sent down the Nile in a picnic basket, and discovered by Pharaoh's daughter. Your birth mother ended up nursing you again, thanks to your big sister. That's quite a bit of drama. But it was just a preview of all the drama that was to come in your adult life.

You became a murderer. You saw one of your people being beaten by an Egyptian, so you killed him and hid the body in the sand. Sand? Really? Didn't you watch *How to Get Away with Murder*? The next day, a fellow Hebrew confronted you about it, so you did the only sensible thing to do in that situation: you ran.

Then one day while you were working your shepherding shift for your father-in-law, God got your attention in a big, dramatic, unexpected way. Ta-da! The burning bush in all its technicolor glory! And He had a mission for you. Go to Pharaoh and tell him to let the Israelites go. Understandably, you started making a few excuses, like, "Lord, who, me? Who exactly am I supposed to say sent me? And God, you know I'm not a good talker, so maybe somebody else needs to take this assignment."

By the way, when He told you to throw down the staff, it became a snake, He told you to grab it by its tail, and it became a staff again, that would have taken me out, totally and completely.

But back to you. You mustered up the courage and went to Pharaoh, and of course he pretty much told you and your brother Aaron to get to steppin'. It took bloody water, frogs, gnats, flies, dead livestock, boils, hail, locusts, darkness, and dead babies to finally get his attention. After all that, he told you and the Israelites, "Good riddance. Don't let the door hit ya where the good Lord split ya."

You even had a dramatic departure. After y'all left, Pharaoh realized he didn't want that free labor walking out the door, so he rounded up his posse and gave chase. But God wasn't finished working miracles through you. Right there at the Red Sea, after you parted it and the Israelites went sashaying through on dry land, you stretched out your hand again, the water came roaring back, and the Egyptians all drowned.

Now, let's move on to your time in the wilderness with that band of complainers. Seriously, whine, whine, whine. I'd like to think I would have had a better attitude. I think …

Let's talk about the Ten Commandments and the tablets. I understand why you got so mad that you broke them. You went away to commune with the Lord and came back to find your people had gone stone-cold crazy. A golden calf, for real? Do better, people.

If people could go back and change history, I'm guessing you'd pick the defining moment where God told you to speak to the rock, and instead what did you do? You hit it not once but twice. Oh, Moses, this is when we'd have some crescendoing movie music right there. So you didn't get to go into the Promised Land. God let you see it, but you didn't get to step foot into it. But your life had a profound impact on us all.

I have this one question: When you broke the tablets, did you try to super-glue them back together before you told God what happened?

Moses's story:

Exodus, Leviticus, Numbers and Deuteronomy

Noah

Hey, Noah. I first read about your story when I was a little girl in Sunday school. I've been rather fascinated with you since then. First of all, I want you to know I never held that drunk incident against you. I know people who've thrown back one too many at one point and done some things they aren't proud of and regretted. For the record, I am not talking about myself. I'm not. Seriously, I'm not.

I always admired your obedience to God. I mean, He told you to do something that people probably made fun of you about it. I'm wondering what the people in your neighborhood said when they saw you building that big boat. I imagine the conversations went something like this.

Them: "Hey, neighbor, whatcha got there?"

You: "It's an ark."

Them: "What's it for?"

You: "It's going to rain."

Them: "Rain?"

You: "Yes, rain."

Them: "I'm president of the HOA. Did you get our permission for this?"

And what about Mrs. Noah? Did she give you the side-eye when you spent so much time working on the ark? The theologians say it took you decades, and you were old at the time. No offense, but you were old.

But I digress.

As a young girl, when I heard your story, I thought it must have been smelly—I mean really smelly—with all those animals aboard with no bathroom facilities for them.

But now, after seeing you face-to-face, I must ask you a very important question: When God told you to bring in animals two by two, do you really think he meant snakes too?

Noah's story:

Genesis 6:5-9:28

Paul

Good afternoon! I'd like to start our conversation by letting you know that when I think of you, two things come to mind. First, you showed us people can change—I mean really change. And second, when God wants to get our attention, He will. You know that better than anyone.

Just think about it. When we first hear about you, you have a different name: Saul of Tarsus. You were a zealot, ruthless, and pretty much a religious terrorist, going around to houses, dragging people out, and putting them in prison. People were probably terrified at just the mention of your name.

But boy, did things turn around that day you were on the road to Damascus with your mind on murder and murder on your mind. All of a sudden, there was a bright light from heaven so powerful that it knocked you to the ground. Then you heard a voice saying, "Saul, why are you persecuting me?" You then asked a logical question: "Who are you?" The voice said, "I'm Jesus. You know, the Jesus you are railing against." Then He told you to go the city and await further instructions. Now, you weren't alone while all this was going on, so I'm sure your traveling companions were trying to figure out what had just happened, why you had fallen to the ground, and whom were you talking to, because they didn't hear a thing. But they had to lead you into the city because this particular incident left you blind—you couldn't see a thing.

Meanwhile in Damacus, the Lord appeared in a vision to Ananias. He was told to go and lay hands on you so you could see again. I bet he was thinking it was a setup. He must have been as nervous as a long-tailed cat in a room full of rocking chairs, but he obeyed God, and your life was never the same. You started your ministry in the local synagogues, talking about Jesus and proclaiming He was the Son of God. I'm sure the people who knew you were popping off with, "I remember when he used to kill believers." "I don't believe he's really changed." "He's lying. He's the same old murderous Saul. Nothing changed but his name."

But God had done something miraculous with you and in you. He even gave you a new name, Paul. You had three major missionary journeys preaching the Gospel. And you certainly knew how to multitask because you burned through a lot of stationery, writing letters. We know them as Romans, 1 and 2 Corinthians, Galatians, Ephesians, Philippians, Colossians, 1 and 2 Timothy, Titus, 1 and 2 Thessalonians, and Philemon. Now that we're in heaven, we can settle once and for all who wrote Hebrews. Did you know shorthand, or did you have one of those little machines the court reporters use?

The bottom line is you were fully and completely committed, on fire for Jesus, talking about Him everywhere and to anybody. The scholars say you traveled ten thousand miles preaching the Good News. Your Fitbit must have gotten quite a step count, and you must have worn out some sandals.

All that preaching got you in trouble too, like the time you and Silas were in Philippi, and you cast a demon out of an enslaved girl. That got you beaten, charged with being a public nuisance, and thrown in the slammer. But even there, you continued to preach. When the earthquake rocked the joint and everybody's chains fell off, even the prison guard gave his life to Christ. Oh, and what about that time you were teaching in the upper room, and that young man fell asleep and fell out the window? I'm sure it was because he was tired and not because you were long-winded and boring. No, not that. Dude was dead until you took him in your arms and brought him back to life.

And you are proof that nobody promised us the Christian journey would be easy. You were beaten, stoned, sent to prison, and shipwrecked at least three times. You survived several attempts to kill you and had a thorn in your flesh. And yet no matter what, you were still faithful and content.

I learned a lot of lessons from you, but I have a lingering question. The thorn in the flesh—was it physical, or people who got on your last nerve? Because if it was people, I totally understand.

Paul in the Bible and his letters:

Acts
Romans
1 Corinthians
2 Corinthians
Galatians
Ephesians
Philippians
Colossians
1 Thessalonians
2 Thessalonians
Philemon
1 Timothy
2 Timothy
Titus

Peter

Oh, hey, it's the rock—the original rock that is. Hello, Peter. I liked reading your story, especially when I messed up. Not to bring up your big failure since we're here in heaven, but …

It all started out so well. You and your brother, Andrew, were at work fishing, and along came big J Himself with a business proposition for you. Quit your job and follow Him, and He would take you fishing for people. Y'all must have been thinking, "So let me get this straight. We're going to cast out a net and catch some actual people in it?" But still without knowing exactly what you were getting yourselves into, you understood the assignment and signed up with Jesus and His merry band of disciples.

It must have been exciting, listening to Jesus teach in the synagogues, preaching the Good News to crowds of people, and healing sick folks, including you very own mother-in-law. I bet after that, she never complained about her son-in-law who gave up his good fishing job, did she?

And the stuff you saw! How about the time Jesus was walking on water, and at first y'all thought he was a ghost? But when you asked Jesus to call you to Him, and He did, you walked on water too. Dude, you walked on water! That is, until you took your eyes off Jesus and saw the wind howling. That was when you started to sink and panic, and Jesus reached out and saved you. This was when Jesus said, "Ye of little faith," and asked why you doubted. But I'd like to point out that at least you got out of the boat.

Now, here's when a whole lot of drama enters your story. Jesus predicted He was going to die. You had a natural reaction and told Him no! Not on your watch. Jesus responded with "Get thee behind me, Satan." Whoa. What was going through your mind right then?

And later, when He predicted you would deny Him, you said, "Even if everybody else bails out on You, Jesus, I've got Your back." Then Jesus said before the rooster says cock-a-doodle-do, you will have denied Him not once, not twice, but three times.

The night when Judas joined the posse to arrest Him, it was you, according to John, who cut off the ear of the high priest's servant. I realize it was wrong of you to do that, but I kinda respect your total gangsta move there.

This was when things get right interesting. While Jesus was on trial in that sham Sanhedrin court, you were in the courtyard. A girl came along and said, "Hey, weren't you with the defendant, Jesus?" You probably had sweaty palms and were stuttering by then, and you said, "Wasn't me." Another young lady came along and pointed out that you were with Jesus. Again you said, "You must have me confused with somebody else. I don't know Him." By this time, a little crowd had gathered around you, and they said you were "one of them" and knew it because of your accent. This time you again said you didn't know Him, and you said it in some rather colorful language. And then ... cock-a-doodle-do. And you were crushed and reduced to tears.

But thanks to you, we get a powerful story about redemption and restoration. After Jesus rose from the dead, one day you were back at your old fishing job. It wasn't going so well until Jesus came along and suggested throwing your net on the right side of the boat. It worked, and you hauled in more fish than the nets could hold. Then after the fish fry, He restored you to the ministry, asking you if you loved Him and sending you out to feed His sheep.

Yes, after everything that happened and how bad you felt, Jesus restored you, assuring you of His love for you and that He could still use you.

You must have been relieved and overwhelmed.

I have one question for you: When you got out of the boat and walked on water, did you take swimming lessons after that?

Moments with Peter:

Matthew 14:22–33
Matthew 26:31–75
Luke 22:31–34
John 13:36–38
John 21
1 Peter
2 Peter

Rahab

Hey, girl. I'm really glad I ran into you today. Yours is such a powerful story about grace and redemption and faith. After all, you are mentioned in Hebrews 11, the Hall of Faith.

But before that, we first read about you when you were in Jericho, working in what's been called the world's oldest profession. How about that? Somebody with a very checkered past ended up in the Hall of Faith. God's power to transform lives is really something, isn't it?

As the Israelites were approaching Jericho and preparing to battle y'all, Joshua sent in two CIA agents to scope out the area. The two spies ended up at your house. Apparently, nobody in town got suspicious of two strange men appearing on your doorstep, considering your profession at that time. Let me say it again: at that time. But there's so much more to your life story.

Anyhoo, despite their cloak-and-dagger operation, the king of Jericho found out spies were within the city and gave orders to find them and bring them to him. The king's henchmen came to your house looking for the spies. But you were fast on your feet and said, "See, what had happened was they were here, yes, but I didn't know where they came from. When it was getting dark, they left. I don't know which way they went. But if you hurry along, you may be able to catch them." However, you fooled them big-time because you had taken the spies onto the roof of your house and hidden them there. Very clever of you.

Later that evening, you had a conversation with the spies and told them everything you had heard about what the Lord had done for the people of Israel. Then you made a bold move and asked them to repay the kindness you'd shown to them. You asked them to spare the lives of your parents, your siblings, and their families. The spies agreed and told you to gather your family in your home and tie a scarlet cord in your window to mark your house.

Sure enough, when the time came, the spies came back to your house and got you and your family safely out of town, before the Israeli army torched Jericho and everything in it.

So you saved your whole family. And not only are you in Hebrews, but you're mentioned by name in the lineage of Jesus! Like I said, your story has redemption written all over it.

Before I depart, one quick question: I'll admit to being a little nosy, but obviously you had to choose a new line of work. What was it?

Rahab's story:

Joshua 2
Joshua 6:22-25

Ruth

Ruth, I must know, is it weird for you now to know that your husband's name became a thing? You know, "finding my Boaz," "praying for my Boaz," and "waiting for my Boaz"? I know there's so much more to you than the man you married, but let's face it: you didn't have to go on *The Bachelorette* or swipe right on Tinder to, well, get your Boaz.

Anyway, let's talk about you. What you did was pretty much awesome sauce. In the grief of losing your first husband, you still had a heart for your mother-in-law and followed her back to her hometown. You must have been such a comfort to her. And girl, didn't our Father lay out some serious blessings for you after that?

There you were in the field, minding your own beeswax, when Boaz noticed you and was obviously smitten because he started trying to find the 411 about you. He was bold enough to step to you and let you know you could stay there in the fields with his workers. You didn't have to worry about sexual harassment on the job because he was serious about company policy. He told his workers to leave you alone. Being a protector is such an attractive quality, wouldn't you say? Then to top it off, he invited you to the company luncheon.

Now, I don't know if you were interested in him by this time, but clearly your mother-in-law, Naomi, knew how to help this relationship along because she sent you to him well prepared.

And it ended like a fairytale: you two got married (was it a big fancy wedding because Boaz was so well-known and wealthy?), you had a baby, and apparently you lived happily ever after. And you were David's great grandma. That's pretty cool.

Before you go, one more question: When you were in the field and Boaz took notice of you, did the other women dress up for work, put on a little makeup, and get their hair done the next day?

Ruth's story:

Ruth

Samaritan Woman at the Well

Hello there. Don't mean to interrupt you, but do you have time for coffee? We need to have a little convo about water, you know, that living water.

You are one of those women whose names we didn't know, but let me tell you, we knew you. In fact, at some point many of us attended a Woman at the Well Women's Conference. So yeah, you were basically a rock star in the world of women's conferences.

Isn't it weird to think about it now? When you got up that morning, you had no idea what that day would bring and the encounter you would have with Jesus Christ Himself.

You were simply trying to get some water from the well, and this man—a Jew, no less—struck up a conversation with you. Of course you were shocked. The Jews didn't even like Samaritans. But this particular fella started chatting you up, talking about God, and asking for a drink of water. Who does that?

He started talking about living water, and you were of course interested. Living water? Why, yes, I think I would like that, thank you very much.

And here's where it gets real interesting. He told you to go get your hubby. When you told him you weren't married, He dropped this little gem: you'd had five husbands and were currently shacked up with a man you weren't married to right then. Gulp!

You recognized He must have been some kind of prophet because He knew all your business. In the conversation that followed, He revealed to you that He was in fact the Messiah. Obviously you were so excited to share the good news with everybody in your village—so excited that you ran off and left your water bucket as well.

I do have one question for you: When you got back home, did you tell the man you were living with, "Hey, let me say this in the nicest way possible … pack your bags and get out. Love ya, mean it"?

The woman at the well's story:

John 4

Samuel

Samuel, you had a lot of jobs. A lot. Judge, priest, prophet, appointer of kings (Saul), anointer of kings (David) … did I leave out any?

And here's a bit of trivia about you. You have two books in the Bible named after you, but in the way it's divided, you're only in one book.

I was very excited to meet your mom, Hannah, the other day. She's one of my favorite people in the Bible. She can tell you all about our conversation later. I always wondered how you felt when she and your dad, Elkanah, dropped you off at the temple and left you in Eli's care. Did you understand that she wasn't abandoning you—she was fulfilling a promise she made to the Lord?

I really admire that you didn't knuckle under to peer pressure while growing up. You didn't pick up any bad habits from Eli's bad sons, who were—let's face it—complete scoundrels, keeping part of the sacrifices for themselves and sexually exploiting women working at the Tabernacle. Yup, losers.

You also gave us a good lesson about listening for the voice of God. One night, you thought it was Eli calling out to you. He told you to go back to bed, listen again, and ask the Lord to speak because His servant was listening. I love that.

It must have been rather frustrating for you to warn the Israelites that they shouldn't want a king. But nooo, they insisted. Be careful what you ask for because they ended up with Saul, and that turned out to be a royally hot mess.

Anyway, it's nice to see you. Before I go, I have a question for you: Were you ever tempted to text your mom and say, "Come get me. Eli's sons are cray-cray"?

Samuel's story:

1 Samuel

Sarah

I'm super glad to see you. There are many things to discuss with you. I'll try not to take up too much of your time, because we have all of eternity to catch up. You had such an interesting and exciting life, but you know when we think of you, the first thing we think is you are Sarah, the woman who had a baby in her nineties.

But before we get to that great miracle, let me get this straight. Abraham came to you one day and said, "Sweetie, pack your bags. We're moving." I'm assuming you asked for details and got something like, "I have no idea where we're going. God's telling us to go, so we're going." No time to get estimates from the movers—you two just packed up the tent, put your stuff on the camel's back, and were on your merry way.

By the way, you are just as stunning as I imagined. I suppose that's why Abraham twice "stretched the truth" and told folks you were his sister, figuring somebody might actually kill him to get to you.

Now, about Hagar. This part of your story is so wild. You came up with this not-so-brilliant idea to have your husband sleep with the maid so he could have a son, and you claimed you'd treat him as your own. Did you have your fingers crossed when you said that? And surprise, surprise, your hubby agreed to your little scheme. Congratulations on keeping that out of the tabloids and away from the paparazzi. Of course, everything changed when she got pregnant and threw it in your face. You got an attitude about the situation, and she ran away. I'm sure looking back on it now, you realize that plan had trouble written on it from the get-go. Oh, yes, I know hindsight is twenty-twenty, and most of us have cooked up a few crazy schemes in our lives.

Then when you were eavesdropping and overheard the conversation that you were going to have a son, you burst out laughing. Who can blame you? You were ninety, well past your childbearing years.

But what joy you must have felt when you finally held baby Isaac in your arms—the physical proof that God can do anything, that nothing is too hard for Him.

I've always wondered: that time when Abraham was going to take Isaac to be sacrificed, did you know what was going on, or did Abe just say, "Hey, the kid and I are going out for a while. Be back later"? I'm thinking that if he spilled the beans, you would have had some choice words for the father of many nations. And then when they returned, was Isaac acting like it was just another father-son day, or did he burst through the front door of the tent with, "Mom! You are never, and I mean never, going to believe what happened today. I need an extra dessert. I almost died"?

Before I let you go, I have this one last question for today: Because you had a baby in your nineties, did you get annoyed when people said, "What a lovely grandson you have"?

Sarah's story:

Genesis 11:27–23:2

Solomon

Good morning, King Solomon. I could have used your wisdom a lot when I needed to make a decision during my Earthly journey. Not only were you wise, but you were wealthy too. Ordinarily this is where I might ask to borrow a few bucks, but no need for money here in heaven. This is fantastic.

You were born into quite the prominent family. Your daddy was King David, and your mother was the lovely Bathsheba. We won't go into details about their relationship. Let's just talk about you.

When you became king, God told you to ask Him for whatever you wanted from Him. Whoa! Anything? Yes, anything. You could have asked for the world's largest fleet of camels, the top goats in all the land, and more shekels than anyone who'd ever lived. But you asked for wisdom. Yes, wisdom. God ended up giving you that and much more.

My favorite story about you is when the two women came before you, each one claiming to be the mother of the same child. Your solution? Well, let's just cut that cute little bundle of joy in half. One half for you, and one half for you. But the real mother said give the baby to the other woman. The fake mom seemed cool with the idea of splitting the baby in two. That was when you made the call: give the baby to the first woman. That was a better ruling than any episode of *The People's Court*.

One thing I'll say for you: you were extravagant in everything you did. First of all, you had seven hundred wives and three hundred concubines. You had thousands of horses and chariots. Your vet bill must have been outrageous. You spent seven years building the first Jewish Temple and thirteen years building your royal palace, and neither one of them was shabby.

Oh, but the apple doesn't fall far from the tree. You and your daddy both had an eye for the ladies, and it got you in trouble. Your foreign wives turned your attention away from God and toward their false gods, rituals, and practices. You even started building buildings for their gods. And our God, the only wise God, was not happy.

But I will say this for you: you wrote about a lot of different stuff. You dropped some pearls of wisdom on us in Proverbs, you got real with us about the meaning of life in Ecclesiastes, and then in Song of Solomon, you talked about S-E-X in a way that's not G-rated for some crowds.

Then after forty years as king and the last king of a unified Israel, you died of natural causes at a ripe old age.

That's a pretty spectacular life. But I have a question: Did you have a spreadsheet to keep up with all the birthdays for the seven hundred wives and three hundred concubines? And you must have really dreaded Valentine's Day.

Solomon's story:

1 Kings 1–11
Song of Solomon/Song of Songs
Proverbs
Ecclesiastes

Stephen

Hi, Stephen. Mind if I sit down and chat for a moment? You had a lot of firsts: first Christian martyr, one of the first deacons in the early Church, and the standard-bearer for what it means to be bold about your faith until the very end, no matter what you faced.

Man, you were on fire for Jesus and spreading the Gospel. Luke described you as a man of faith and of the Holy Spirit, full of grace and power. You were a Christian revolutionary, and it got you in big-time trouble with some of the Jewish leaders who were worried people might actually listen to your message and start following this Jesus character.

Some people told some enormous lies about you and falsely claimed you were blaspheming both God and Moses. That got you hauled into the Sanhedrin Council's kangaroo court on those trumped-up charges. Here's what I've wanted to know: those in the courtroom could see that your face was like the face of an angel, but that didn't faze them. Make it make sense.

You totally schooled them with the longest speech in the book of Acts. Your impassioned defense was flawless, laying out Israelite history and their rejection of those sent to lead them. And of course the Jewish leaders couldn't handle the truth, and an angry mob of council members dragged you outside the city and stoned you to death.

But before you passed on to glory, you had this vision of Jesus at the right hand of God. And as you were being stoned, this was when we knew for certain that you were the real deal Holyfield in your faith. You asked God not to hold that sin against them. They were killing you, and you were saying, "Lord, don't hold it against them."

If that was a TV show, it would have made a great season cliffhanger. The camera would pan over to a man in the crowd who's the coat checker for the killers. . And that man is none other than—cue the dramatic music—Saul. Yes, that Saul. Saul of Tarsus.

It's getting late, and I have some heavenly errands to run, but before I go, a question: What happened to the other deacons? Nobody came to court to be your character witness?

Stephen's story:

Acts 6–7

Woman with the Issue of Blood

Glad I finally caught up with you. I love how you hang out in a crowd now. I was trying to get your attention, and then I realized something. I couldn't call you by name because we never knew your name. But I know your story, and I'm honored to meet you.

I can't imagine all you went through: a medical condition that caused your bleeding for twelve years—not twelve hours or even twelve days or twelve months, but twelve long years. You must have been physically and emotionally exhausted. You went from doctor to doctor, and they could never find out what was wrong with you or make you better. In fact, you got worse. That had to be so frustrating.

I can imagine how you must have felt that day when you heard Jesus was in town. Finally, help just might be on the way after all those years of suffering. I know you didn't feel well, but just the thought of getting well probably had you doing a little two-step while you were getting dressed.

And props to you for your courage and determination. You knew there would be a rock concert–sized crowd around Jesus, but that didn't stop you. And here's the thing: you made your way through the crowd, probably saying, "Pardon me, excuse me," all the way. This is the Amazon Prime movie part. You slowly made your way through the throng of people, you were trying to be discreet, and you got closer and closer until there He was: Jesus. You were right there with the Great Healer, the Great Physician. And you reached out and touched the hem of his garment. Then, miracle of all miracles, the bleeding stopped. It was gone. You immediately felt better and stronger. But before you could shout hallelujah, Jesus felt someone had touched Him, and He wanted to know who did it. Peter chimed in with, "Jesus, there are beaucoup people out here. Anybody could have touched you." But no, Jesus insisted some healing power had flowed from Him, and He wants to know who got it. So even though your hands were most likely trembling, you stepped forward, kneeled at his feet, identified yourself, and told Him your whole medical story. (Even though He knew all about you.)

Then in front of God and the whole world, He lovingly called you "daughter" and said you took a risk to trust Him, and it paid off because your faith made you well. That's an ending worthy of a big fireworks display.

I have a question for you: What's your name?

The woman's story:

Matthew 9:20–22
Mark 5:25–34
Luke 8:43–48

Epilogue

I had all these questions I planned to ask you when I saw You face-to-face. I thought I'd ask You about some of the great mysteries of our times and about some of the things that didn't work out the way I had wanted them to. I thought I would have a million questions for You when I got to the pearly gates. I was all ready for a big ol' heart-to-heart with You.

But now that I'm here, and now that I see you and see heaven, I just want to say, Lord, Jesus, Holy Spirit, thank you!

Acknowledgments

Thanks to those who've been on this book journey with me, providing valuable feedback, making suggestions, cheering me on, and encouraging me to quit dragging my feet and finish it. Thanks to Angela King, Jacqueline Randolph, and Brian Shields, who read along as I wrote many of the chapters and told me to keep writing. Thanks to Rick Brunson, a fellow lover of the written word who said he could hear my voice. When I heard that, I knew I couldn't quit.

About the Author

Vanessa Echols is an award-winning journalist who spent forty years as a television news anchor covering major local and national stories. She is the winner of three regional Emmy Awards and the recipient of a Florida Association of Broadcast Journalists award for a podcast on the 1920 massacre in the town of Ocoee, Florida. She is also the winner of a Black Podcasting Award and an Anthem Award for her podcast, *Colorblind: Race across Generations.*

CPSIA information can be obtained
at www.ICGtesting.com
Printed in the USA
JSHW050214250822
29636JS00002B/100